Retail fashion procurement team roles and processes

Charles Nesbitt

Copyright and ISBN 1543162320

Also by Charles Nesbitt

FUNDAMENTALS FOR SUCCESSFUL AND SUSTAINABLE FASHION BUYING AND MERCHANDISING

*

FUNDAMENTALS FOR FASHION RETAIL STRATEGY PLANNING AND IMPLEMENTATION

*

FUNDAMENTALS FOR FASHION RETAIL ARITHMETIC, ASSORTMENT PLANNING AND TRADING

*

FUNDAMENTALS OF FASHION RETAIL, TECHNOLOGY, MANUFACTURING AND SUPPLIER MANAGEMENT

*

THE COMPLETE JOURNAL OF FASHION RETAIL BUYING AND MERCHANDISING

Contents

PREFACE

The process of buying and selling in some form or other of goods has been with us since time immemorial. Often when one stands in bewilderment in an elegant shopping mall and wonder how all the stores are able to effectively seduce the many shoppers trawling the wide corridors to readily part with their well-earned money while at the same time enabling them to possibly enjoy a wonderful social experience.

The plan of offering goods to the potential customer is a complicated one and is a science that involves many players whose individual contributions slot seamlessly together and are so perfectly co-ordinated that it provides the perception that it is the result of one individual concerted effort.

It will be illustrated as to how the relationships of the major functions that intertwine from the conceptualisation of a product through to the presentation of a finished garment to the potential customer and in doing this demonstrates how the key areas such as buying, merchandising, technology, production, design, logistics and selling each with their unique specialised operations manage to achieve this.

INTRODUCTION

Retailing

Retailing is the offer of goods or services for sale by individuals or businesses to an end user. The channels by which these goods reach the final user may vary considerably and arrive via different sources such as wholesalers, trading houses or directly from the manufacturer and there are equally many differing variants in the way the goods are put on sale. Historically it is more likely that shopping would have been done at the village or town market, in a high street shop or at the "mom and pop" store which evolved over time into mass retailing stores that are often housed in shopping malls supported by smaller line shops.

More recently with the advent of the computer utilising various platforms such as the internet or social networks, shopping on line is growing exponentially using electronic payment methods with delivery via the post or with a courier man knocking on the front door of the customer bearing their purchase relatively shortly after the transaction has been processed.

The products that are put on offer will be determined by the demand to satisfy a need in the market place. Broadly the merchandise may be categorized into food stuffs, hard or durable goods such as appliances, furniture and electronics and soft goods that have a limited life span typically clothing, apparel and fabrics. Whatever the nature of the product, the key objective will be to acquire and sell the product at a price that will be more than it cost to bring it to the place of offer and thereby make a profit.

Supporting activities such as the storage, movement of the goods, technology, and marketing will endeavour to ensure that the form, function and profit objective is maximised.

In an effort to put in perspective the activities and interaction between the various functional players and their dependency and integration with each other for the end to end process of the product workflow is broadly depicted in the diagram below

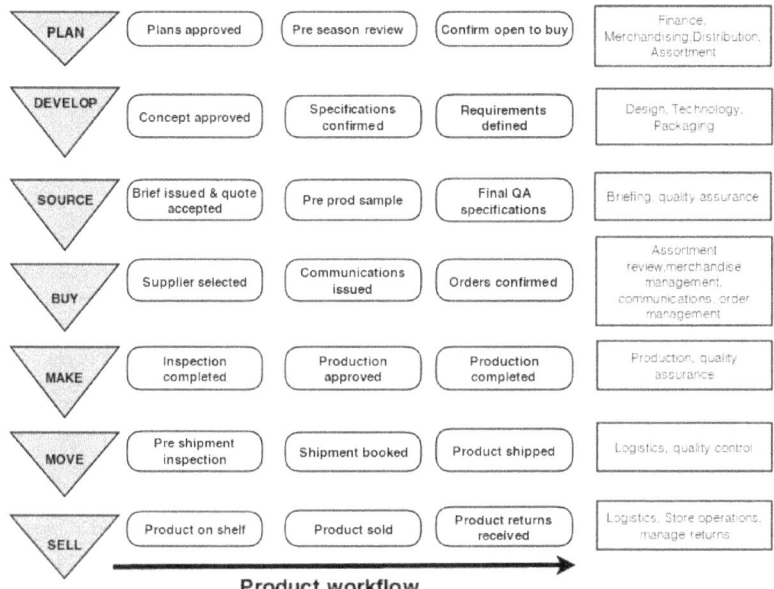

Product workflow

The distinction between supply chain and value chain should be clarified in that it is frequently misunderstood and the interpretation is varied.

Simply put, the supply chain is the processes and activities that take place from conceptualisation of styles through to the procurement of raw materials and production process to the logistical operations and the eventual delivery to the end user. The value chain component is the inclusion of those functions that support the supply chain process such as the marketing philosophies, human resource management, and consultancy resources.

The intimate details of the roles will be exposed in the future sections as the science of retailing is explored in greater detail.

The retail players

The saying "no man is an island" holds true in many spheres and this is certainly the case in the world of clothing retailing.

Various players, each with very different specialised skills are amalgamated together to deliver a completed outcome which is that of presenting product for sale to potential customers. These players are often very diverse not only in the activities that they perform but also in their personality traits which they possess. The key to a successful team is how maturely the interaction takes place and the mutual respect that every member has for each other's roles.

Below is a brief synopsis of the main player's roles and their dependency and integration with each other.

THE PROCUREMENT TEAM

The foremost players in the clothing and apparel procurement team consist typically of the following members and are described in broad terms.

Designers

Designers have a deep insight into the market they are targeting through the analysis of the changing trends and use these to provide creative direction and develop product designs for the buying teams to consider.

Usually these participants tend to think out of the box and their creative minds can challenge some of the comfort zones of other team members. What must be kept top of mind is that they need to consistently apply their intellect way ahead of time as to what they think the customer requires as opposed to their personal desires.

Typically the character traits which they will possess are that they are independent, spontaneous, extroverts, driven by ideas and are confident by nature.

Although the general perception of the word "designer" conjures up a vision of those who work at couture level, the reality is that it also includes those who are involved in creating ranges which may also be exclusive but will be more widely available and therefore can be considered as having been mass produced. Their choices will be influenced by the type of retailer they work for or the product category that they design for. The more traditional retailer which serves predominantly mature customers will be less influenced by radical fashion swings which in contrast will definitely affect the younger market's high fashion boutiques more rigorously.

Work is done at times under enormous pressure to meet critical deadlines, tough meeting schedules and involves frequent international travel. It is not surprising the perception is often one that they live a life of glory and glamour but contrary to this belief the reality is that it is not as extravagant as made out to be.

The fashion and trade shows, whether they be for yarn, fabric or garments are tiring affairs requiring hard work and stamina as is the shopping for appropriate samples, researching fashion magazines, the use of forecasting trend agencies, internet and blogs and out of all of this they need to possess the ability to then distil the emerging trends to create a storybook that will best suit their organisation's customer profiles.

The designer lives with the constant strain of knowing that their level of success will be measured by the eventual amount of money rung up at the till and getting the styling direction wrong or overextending the life of a particular look could have severe financial implications, especially in the cases where volumes are high.

The real challenge is to convince the buying teams and senior management to buy into their vision and have the confidence that what they have in mind will be commercially acceptable to the customer. The designer cannot ignore the technical aspects of the garment production as many problems can be evaded if these are taken cognisance of during the design process.

Retailers in the southern hemisphere do have the advantage that their seasons follow those of countries in the northern hemisphere which allows them to tap into the more successful designs that are trading in volume. However, with globalisation this is not always as clear cut as it was in previous years and the ability to follow as close to the season as possible requires techniques that facilitates the shortening of lead times and attempt to get the product to market as quickly as possible. The advent of communication technologies such as satellite television, internet and social media have brought exposure to different cultures, sports, films, lifestyles and trends such as those generated by specific events, health drives, environmental awareness and technology platforms that can have significant impacts on fashion which sometimes happen at very short notice.

A very important aspect is that the designer must adhere strictly to, is that of copyright. Instances have occurred that other competitor's garments are copied almost identically whether it be by style, print or design. Invariably the driving reason for this is the speed of being able to turn on a replica at a cheaper price. Although it may not be practical to register and copyright every design, any infringement can still be challenged and a consequence could occur of having the offending garments being removed from display and destroyed.

Design briefs are made up of significant trend and brand information which are constructed by the design team that include information such as anticipated key silhouettes within the assortments and colour themes, fabric types, print influences and technical direction which will be distributed to buying, planning, technology and sourcing teams.

The brief takes the form of a presentation with the use of story boards and flow charts with description of the themes.

Design concept workshops are set up with relevant stakeholders that may or may not include suppliers with appropriate samples, materials and artwork out of which seasonal concept story boards will evolve by department or brand that will depict the expected themes, key looks for the season, colour palettes, styles and fabric types that will be dominant

A simple example of a typical story board ladies fashion highlighting looks, colour pallette, fabrics and themes is illustrated below

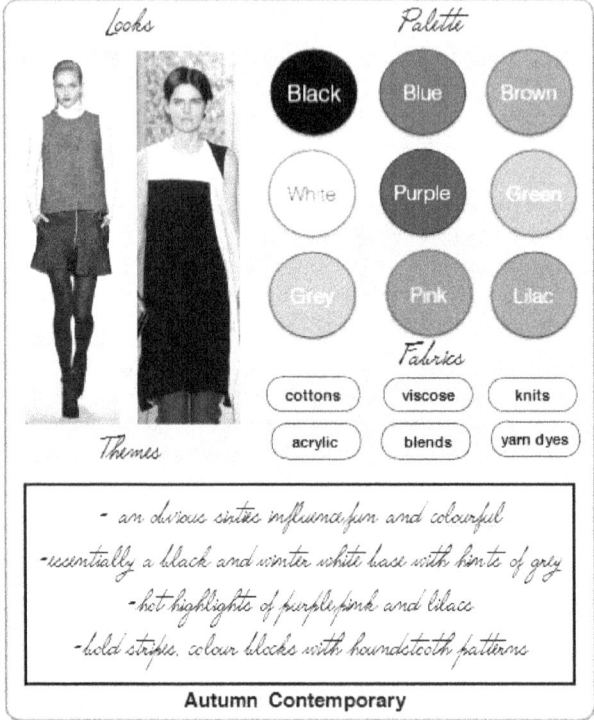

After the design brief is completed and is signed off by the senior management team, buying, design and trend teams commence the conducting of product workshops.

Trends, insights and fads

Trends and insights indicate as to where your brand currently is and ideally where it should be. They are used to guide your decision making and help in the formulation of the strategy until the whole picture evolves.

The trend can be best described as the general direction how the consumer buying behaviour is developing and is changing and therefore has no beginning and has no end as it provides indicators in the development of the brand.

Trends are driven by attributes such as a specific look, a lifestyle, colour, fabric, style, a shape or innovation. It is crucial that a trend is accepted by the target customer in that they need to understand and embrace the trend as well as the fact that the style can be adapted for mass appeal. The trend must be able to be accommodated in the existing price structure and have an acceptable amount of risk that will blend into the overall range. It is therefore really important that to minimise the risk that the trends have to be identified as those that have staying power and have the potential of becoming profitable and that the strategy can be adapted in order that they are in accordance with emerging trend data so as to match the customers' needs , wants and desires.

It is important to note that trends are not necessarily continually on an increment, some explode and become relevant while others disappear. They are also not created in isolation as they are influenced by social and environmental factors which will have an effect on various industries, individuals, companies' products and services which makes the harvesting of accurate data paramount.

An insight differs in that it comprises of accurate understanding and intuitive analysis of the person or thing that is served. In other words it is the "why", and 'what if" and so it therefore depends on creative thinking and analysis.

There is often confusion in the distinction as to what is a trend and that which is a fad. To distinguish between the two, a trend is a popular general direction which takes longer to build than a fad and lasts longer for which there is a bigger demand. The fad generally has a smaller demand and seldom migrates into the mainstream and characteristically generates a very high rate of interest for a very short period of time and is often just a flash in the pan. To draw a comparison, belted waists for dresses may be seen as a trend for an entire season or longer but "oncies" all in one fleece garments for men were a fad that did not last very long.

It is therefore understandable that the implementation of trends, insights and fads can be considerably complex but eventually the objective through the integration of the three elements is to through being innovation and steady management to provide a nimble, agile and flexible business plans, marketing strategies, brand development, and organisational structures within a constantly changing operational environment.

Product workshops aim to build a balanced assortment for the season which is aligned to the strategies as set down and meet the range summary.

In these workshops the following will take place

- Samples, artwork and prototypes will be reviewed and approved or rejected
- The colour palettes will be set across the customer segmentations, core continuity products and fashion assortments
- The continuity, core and input items will be confirmed
- Gaps or outstanding items will be identified for which appropriate designs need to sourced

The volumes per customer choice at sub class level is provided by the planning arm and the buyer will decide which product will be assigned to the choice option.

Buyers

The buyer needs to have a clear understanding of the product that is required which is in line with the trend guidelines best suited to their target customer profiles, for both the high fashion segment as well as those that best serve the more traditional customer.

It is a fact is that the role of the designer and the buyer may be a bit blurred in that they research the same fashion forecasting sites and other sources of inspiration in order to put a range of garments together. Both roles must be aware of sizing, quality and costs related to fabrics, trimmings and production. To achieve this successfully they must be flexible enough to develop and buy the most suitable product that is in line with the prescribed strategy and achieves the desired profit margin in keeping with the set down targets. The evaluation of competitive activity and product ranges through regular store visits and comparative shopping provides the knowledge required to keep ahead of the field.

Effective communication and presentation skills are a prerequisite to brief and interact with suppliers as well as presenting product reviews to colleagues within their own group at all levels of seniority. With this comes the need to be able to accept criticism and resolve problems in a mature manner. The sad fact is that frequently when the analysis of the success of the range is evaluated at the end of the season, if the results are disappointing it is not uncommon for the buyer to shoulder the emotional burden of the poor performance. The truth of the matter is that the range was presented on more than one occasion to all team players including senior management all of whom signed the range off but in the final analysis they are more often than not, as is human nature, reluctant to be accept any proper accountability.

Coupled to ability to understand the wants of the customer is the sourcing of the most suitable supplier that will be selected for the specified product types in terms of their particular skills, technical ability, costing efficiency, attitude, transparency, honesty, focus on quality, communications and competitiveness while still meeting the ethical criteria that are acceptable to society.

A large part of the task will be to maintain good relations with suppliers, while at the same time being able to assertively negotiate prices with them and make sure the planned stocks are delivered on time. Communications need to be clear and specific to avoid disputes over issues which may arise through vague and confusing messages. For these reasons they need to be confident, take decisions based on results and be driven by a sense of urgency.

The buyer has to be multi-talented in that as well as being creative they also need to monitor the sales objectively and be flexible enough to react accordingly in terms of turning on or turning off production and transferring fabric and components to more appealing product styles where sales performance and fast emerging trends dictate.

What is key to be a successful buyer is the ability to work as part of the overall team and influence the rest of the team's activities which could be in the form of a managerial and developmental capacity that could also include both their peers and superiors.

The display of emotional maturity and commercial acumen within the controlled parameters as set by the merchandising arm in terms of the budgets, the number of product options and display space constraints is absolutely essential.

The same principle applies to the relationships that need to be maintained with the technical teams in regard to the use of the most appropriate fabrics which meet the product form and function demands in addition to ensuring that the brand standards of the garment are observed.

The fact that potentially the buyer together with the other retail players will be dealing with three to four seasons simultaneously at different stages for each season makes their task even more complicated. To clarify the phenomenon a bit further, the journey of this book attempts to describe the process from beginning to end for one season but while trading in the current season the thoughts and strategies are being developed and documented for two or possibly three seasons ahead followed by the range development leading up to the production taking place for next upcoming season.

The ability to absorb and interpret vast amounts of information from various sources, much of which originates from complex IT systems, can present a challenge to those who are not analytically minded. Systems have altered the scope of the traditional buyer from being a pure "touchy feely art skill" to having to develop basic technical abilities through the continual emergence of innovative systems which have become a great advantage to the role.

Some buyer's, such as those for knitwear, ladies structured underwear, tailoring and footwear will require more expert fabric and garment construction knowledge of their respective industries in comparison to individuals who select the more straightforward cut, make and trim products such as dresses, blouses and casual trousers.

As the trade environment has become more global and through information technology development it is much faster, interactive and has enabled business to be done more effortlessly from a home base interacting with many different countries. A great deal of the job is done amongst many new emerging countries which has led to a need for urgency and nimbleness in order to locate the most effective plants that meet the quality requirements, be able to assess the required technical abilities, understand the economic and cultural demands of the respective countries as well as the logistical peculiarities and government regulations that may exist.

The sourcing of production has to take on different approaches as the pros and cons of dealing internationally needs to be carefully weighed up against those of dealing with the ever diminishing number of local suppliers. A critical factor is that suppliers must be ethical in terms of labour practices, remuneration, waste management, working conditions and safety. If such conditions are not met it is counter to the interests of the retailer to be associated with such suppliers from both a moral point of view and the exposure of malpractices could lead to negative media reports and the retailer will suffer the consequences that accompany such deeds. The measurement of performance is therefore key to gauging the effectiveness of suppliers.

In larger organisations a buyer will probably be supported by an assistant or trainee buyer who will normally be a person who wishes to pursue a career in the field. They will be largely responsible for the organisation of the ranges, perform some clerical work whilst preparing products for garment reviews, monitoring the product development critical path and production milestones, liaising with suppliers and technology as well as deputising for the buyer when they are out of the office.

A point to note is that the relationship between buyers and suppliers often develops into more than a pure business association due to the fact that they spend much time travelling together and working closely with one another building ranges. Close familiar relationships frequently make it difficult to maintain a business like association for the mutual benefit of both parties and can cloud business decision making and judgment. The temptation of bribery and incentives in exchange for placing large orders may be desirous. For newer naïve buyers the rule that the supplier is not your friend should be firmly applied simply because they are more easily seduced by grandiose lunches and gifts as many have unfortunately found out the hard way when they move on and are no longer of great importance to the particular supplier.

A way of balancing the workloads or ranking of buyers and merchandisers is to evaluate the actual number of suppliers, stock keeping units or barcodes being handled by each buyer and then make comparisons regarding workload and productivity of each buyer to established benchmarks.

Merchandisers

There is a novelty t-shirt on the market which has the following statement blazon across the front panel which reads as follows – *"Merchandise Planner – we do precision guesswork based on unreliable data by those of questionable knowledge".* Although the humour can be appreciated it should be known that this statement is not too far from the truth as the success of merchandising objectives is reliant on many diverse inputs.

The merchandiser or planner applies their focus on maximising profitability from the business end. This is done largely through the analysis of historical sales and the influence of the trend direction to determine the range categories and product breakdown within the overall sales budget.

The role defines what stock levels are required to meet the preset targets such as seasonal stock turnover or forward stock covers based on the sales trends over time. Knowing these requirements, the merchandiser will determine what intake or purchase quantities are needed at any point in time in the season for the total department and each product category.

The level of the budgets will determine the quantity of options in relation to styling, colour palette, size spans, pricing structure and levels of quality per category that will best service the customer for the time that the goods are expected be on offer prior to a new variety of product being introduced in line with the strategic predetermined seasonal themes.

The merchandiser's job has to be to provide guidance to the buyer to procure within the budget parameters. In short it can be described as providing the buyer with a shopping list or range plan that allows them to go out and fill in the blanks on the plan while buying product. This activity requires the careful management of the "open to buy" which can often be a source of tension between the buyer who always tends to want more and the merchandiser who holds the purse strings. A good deal of emotional maturity and teamwork on both sides is therefore critical for a successful partnership.

Sadly the merchandising role is often branded as a dull, boring number crunching task in accordance with mathematical calculations and while it is this, it can be better described as the creative manipulation of numbers. This task is highly rewarding when positive trade results are achieved or alternatively equally depressing when these do not materialise. The role can be likened to that of a husband who places his entire salary on a dead cert horse at the races which was by no means appreciated by his wife. However when the horse won he was similarly unpopular for not putting more money on the horse!

As it is with the buying role, the merchandiser deals with different activities simultaneously as part of the team across a number of seasons and therefore requires high levels of multi-tasking and re-prioritising in the forward planning, problem resolution, critical milestone management, analysis and timeous action implementation.

As the actual trade takes place the results need to be carefully analysed and immediate action plans initiated in order to maximise the opportunities and minimise the levels of markdowns that erode the profits. For these reasons they need to be logical, reliable, and consistent in order to take decisions based on fact.

The regular timeous generation of reports detailing sales analysis, stock levels and forward planning needs are distributed to all team members and to senior management. Often numeric information and commercial analysis is demanded on an immediate ad-hoc basis which adds pressure to the job function and can be very disruptive to routines which in such situations requires the merchandiser to adapt quickly and effectively.

The merchandiser plays an integral role during the presentation at product reviews from the numbers perspective which influences the agreed product mix and justification of the levels of sales budgets.

 A detailed understanding is necessary of the stores and the customer profile inherent to respective stores that are best met through the attributes of the ranges in terms of styling, colour and size that are put on offer within the store space constraints. The task is best described by the saying "plan each store as if it is your own" which could never be truer.

With sophisticated IT development and the availability of various software packages, some of which may be developed exclusively for the retailer, will provide quick sales analysis, production planning and afford the ability to make sound decisions based on accurate data. This information is especially necessary to give guidance to the allocator or distributor who will be sending the appropriate quantities to satisfy the store's needs as well as give direction as to the level of repeat buys for products that are trading above expectations.

Some organisational structures do differentiate the allocation function between the merchandiser who focuses on the forecasting and production planning and that of the allocator or location planner who will be responsible to distribute the product to the stores in the most appropriate combinations of styles, colour and sizes that meet the store profiles. This function can be housed as an extension within the buying division or may be part of a separate centralised group where an allocator may be responsible for a diverse number of departments. The benefits of such a centralised structure is that there could be a cost saving advantage especially where smaller departments do not warrant a dedicated staff member but added to this is a pool of knowledge which develops a highly skilled team who are able to cross pollinate information, coordinate inter departmental promotions effectively and develop consistent techniques and skills. The identification of common emerging trends will contribute to the optimisation of sales and assist in the control of stock quantities at a very detailed level and thereby maximise profits. Close connections to the departmental merchandisers is maintained to ensure that their actions are aligned to the departmental strategy and plans.

The need for the diversification of the function also makes more sense from the point of view in that where the distribution function is retained within the department it inevitably adds to the increasing workload of the merchandiser. The departmental merchandiser task has more and more been impacted on by the development, the implementation and mastering of complex and sophisticated information systems that analyse sales and stock with added forward planning functionalities.

Many such systems are able to integrate with other supporting IT platforms such as supplier performance, technological measurement, critical path management, ordering, logistical and store systems. The added management of a complex allocation system that is necessary to move the stock to stores is more and more difficult with the result that the incumbent is in danger of being drawn into concentrating on and coping with the intricate detail. As a result, the merchandiser runs the risk of losing sight of the bigger objectives as set out in the strategy and operational plans and the consequent degrading of the inherent merchant intuition becomes very real.

The merchandiser needs to effectively manage and develop the merchandising team which can, not unlike the buying role, consist of an assistant merchandiser or trainee who aspire to be a merchandiser.

The role ensures cohesion of activities that have to be synchronized based on actual sales performance through the formalised interaction with other stakeholders such as the buyers and technologists. This contact is usually in the form of regular, typically weekly, departmental meetings where corrective decisions and plans of action are agreed. Frequent association with the points of sale in stores through written communications and reports as well as formal site visits are critical to keep aligned with the customer's preferences and emerging trends and confirm that the stores are sharing the same vision of the overall strategy.

The need to guide suppliers assertively in terms of prioritisation and the achievement of deadlines is critical to meet the suitable stock requirements at any point in time, particularly in relation to peak seasonal periods or key events. For example, once winter breaks, which it does every year except the exact date is not easy to predict, the objective is to have the right stocks in place such as knitwear, thermal underwear, scarves and the like in sufficient quantities to meet the rush. The usual manner to assist in the anticipation of the weather trend is done through reference to previous years data when the weather changes happened which also help to understand variations in out of ordinary performance at particular times. The challenge is therefore to have the appropriate quantities in the stores at the vital time while the maintenance of the balance of stocks must be adequate to cater for the demand without overstocking the stores ahead of planned stock targets. Events such as Easter, Christmas, Valentine's Day and Mother's day are easier to predict and the right levels of stock can be made more accurately available at the right time.

Where suppliers do not meet the required delivery dates, the merchandiser needs to manage the consequences that have to be applied for the underperformance. This can result in some very sensitive and emotional discussions and the negotiation of penalties typically in the form of discounts, sale or return agreements or even total cancellation which will no doubt impact negatively on both parties.

Negotiating

Negotiation is the process whereby through dialogue between two or more parties an agreement is met and the outcome satisfies the needs of both within the boundaries that the situation will allow.

In the retail environment, negotiations typically revolve around topics such as price, garment content, costs, innovation and profitability. The discussions can take place under high pressure where the expectations of both parties are elevated and the rivalry is intense. Often the relationship may be under threat which may or may not add another dimension depending how significant the association is. The opposite of this can be, and the most suitable, where the two parties collaborate to reach the most desired outcome.

To achieve a situation where both parties benefit, requires maturity, a clear understanding of the end objectives with informed discussions by both parties and the development of a plan to achieve a mutual objective.

Notwithstanding the above the supplier and the retailer will still have their own agendas. The supplier will wish to sell as much as he can for the best price while the retailer will want the product for as cheap as possible for the best quality. If the retailer does not have an insightful understanding of the manufacturing process the chances are that they might end up paying too much or sacrificing content.

Negotiating can be a traumatic experience and not all may have the appetite for the heightened discussion. In the case of the supplier there could be a tendency to avoid the confrontation and at times simply give the product to the retailer for the price requested, while the retailer, on the other hand, will similarly pay the supplier's more expensive proposal without exploring all options to get the best deal.

The retailer must always be well prepared with all relevant facts regarding fabric, trim, ratings and costs, prevailing exchange rate trends, wage structures, margin policies including other external and internal factors at hand in order to be able to have an informed sincere discussion. The persuasion process must be done in a way that the argument is convincing and the acceptance by the other party is seen to be mutually beneficial, trustworthy and incorporates the other participant's needs.

The progression of negotiation follows the steps of preparation, conducting the discussion and reviewing the outcomes.

Thorough preparation is critical which requires that the issues and opportunities are identified, prioritised and have a value for both parties. Focus must be on both the hard subjects such as the monetary issues and volumes as well as the softer matters such as perceptions.

Boundaries must be set in the types of outcome broken up into which would ideally like to be achieved, or what is likely to be achieved and thirdly the bare minimum that would be accepted.

Analysis of the environment of both businesses must be well defined in terms of the markets, competitor activities and the supplier capability and technical expertise required. These factors coupled to the trading history and what percentage the supplier is of the retailer's business and what the retailer represents of the supplier's total production or put differently, who needs who the most.

Past performance and consistency as well as the growth potential and the degree of product uniqueness or cost advantages are important leverage factors that are to be taken into consideration.

Key bargaining points for the retailer are cost prices, discounts, volumes, exclusivity, return policies, promotional support, delivery scheduling and any other unique service while the supplier's focus is likely to be the volumes that can be achieved, the highest cost price that will be agreed and the long term sustainability of regular business.

There is not always a satisfactory resolution to negotiation discussions and contingency plans need to be in place as to what alternatives are available should a deadlock situation be reached. These may include the possibility of moving production to different suppliers, reduce volumes and increasing the levels of other substitution ranges, the consideration of sale or return agreements and although not desirable, possibly increasing the selling price above the norm.

Behaviour and strategies during the meeting are extremely important. Asking for more than is expected will give room for negotiation to what is acceptable without simply accepting the first offer. It is also essential to remain flexible and creative in an effort to avoid a deadlock situation. A vital point to bear in mind is that at all costs to avoid haggling as this practice runs the risk of destroying a relationship.

If confrontation does transpire, it should be tactically done and at all costs does not include any personal attack or involve the use of threats and ultimatums. The power of silence should be remembered as it can be effective and if needs be, try and concede to small bits at a time, park potentially unresolvable issues even if it means that the meeting has to be temporarily adjourned.

There are personal factors that can influence the final negotiation. Different partakers follow different processes, they have diverse experience levels as well as possess varying understandings and personality traits which may be unpredictable.

There is an added complexity in dealing with off shore suppliers where there are duties, logistical challenges, and culture and language differences.

Once the negotiations are concluded, a documented summary of the agreements, commitment of resources, capacity to deliver and action plans is absolutely critical to ensure complete understanding. The record will enable an amicable resolution should any misinterpretation which could possibly become a point of dispute at a later stage.

Technology

Technical Teams consist broadly of the fabric and garment technologists. Fabric technologists are highly trained specialists who focus on typically woven or knitted disciplines. Specialised products such as knitwear, tailoring and footwear require added knowledge of components and specific production machinery.

A major portion of the fabric technologist's task is the development and innovation of new fabrics and the enhancement of existing products. New fibres and blends of fibres such as the blending of natural and synthetic fibres, addition of chemicals to finishing process will possibly lead to new inventions and improvements such as better washability, softer handles, easy care properties like easy to iron, crease resistant finishes, rot resistant applications, seamless or seams that are glued that allow for smoother looks particularly for under garments, the evolvement of elastane products such as lycra which revolutionised active and casual wear and the enhancement of thermal properties of winter undergarments. The success of such developments which add to the profitability as well as the form and function necessitates a close working relationship with suppliers, mills and value adders.

Garment technology have the responsibility to ensure that the make-up of the garment meets the set down criteria and the componentry like buttons, interlinings and threads are of the standard that is functional and are not inferior.

Many factories have developed specified technological capabilities that have been built around the production of a particular category of garments relevant to them which vary from factory to factory or even within the same plant. The garment technologist must understand this implicitly and exploit this knowledge to its fullest.

The relationship with the commercial team is sometimes strained as the ideal level of form and function can be challenged by the need to market the product at the most commercially competitive price.

The objective of the garment technologist is to ensure that product quality is not compromised. The tasks essential to achieve this can be varied, for example, the assessment of potential manufacturers and fabric mills to ensure that the established standards are achievable, the specification of raw materials, overseeing sampling stages and ensuring that any delays which may result through the process do not compromise the delivery prerequisites.

In safeguarding that the all quality standards are met particularly through the inspection of garments, inspectors need to possess specific skills. Quality controllers should be ethical, sincere and honest, open mindedly being willing to consider alternatives, be diplomatic and tactful in their dealings with people and are able to actively observe their surroundings as well as perceive and adapt to varying situations.

The technologist has an intimate knowledge of the supplier base through historical awareness as well as from continually researching new and existing suppliers. As the sourcing specialist they have to guide buying teams in the selection of the most appropriate manufacturer for the various types of product. It is also very essential that they are conscious of the fabric prominence for the forthcoming season as dictated by the strategies and budget levels to ensure that there is sufficient capacities at the relevant mills to meet the overall demands without compromising quality.

The task of assessing potentially new suppliers is a role that may be included in the stable of the technical team or it may be hived off to defined sourcing specialists who are knowledgeable team members that recognise the strengths and weaknesses of suppliers and based on this where best to place orders accordingly.

Suppliers are assessed on various criteria such as their management infrastructure, financial stability, specialised equipment availability, fabric specialty, levels of innovation, fashion or basic production orientation, the other retailers they serve, their flexibility of cost negotiability and social responsibility policies. Other external factors that may well influence the selection of suppliers could be those like prevailing exchange rates, remuneration policies and physical locality.

In summary, the significance must be emphasised that the diverse buying teams all have to have a clear informed understanding of each other's roles and priorities and that they are aligned to ensure all their tasks are integrated to achieve the goal of delivering consistent quality products manufactured by appropriately skilled suppliers on time all the time. This is especially imperative in the case of more complex products such as corsetry, tailored garments and knitwear.

The handling, packaging, storage and movement of the product through the supply channels has to be done in such a way that the quality of the product is not allowed to deteriorate in any way whatsoever. As some product is sourced from more distant locations a newer trend is to contract the technical function out to approved independent technical service providers or to trusted garment and fabric suppliers themselves who understand and are committed to the standards required. These service providers are thereby able to approve samples, perform quality control and be responsible for the eventual release of the finished product.

The responsibilities of the main participants in the product workshop is illustrated as follows

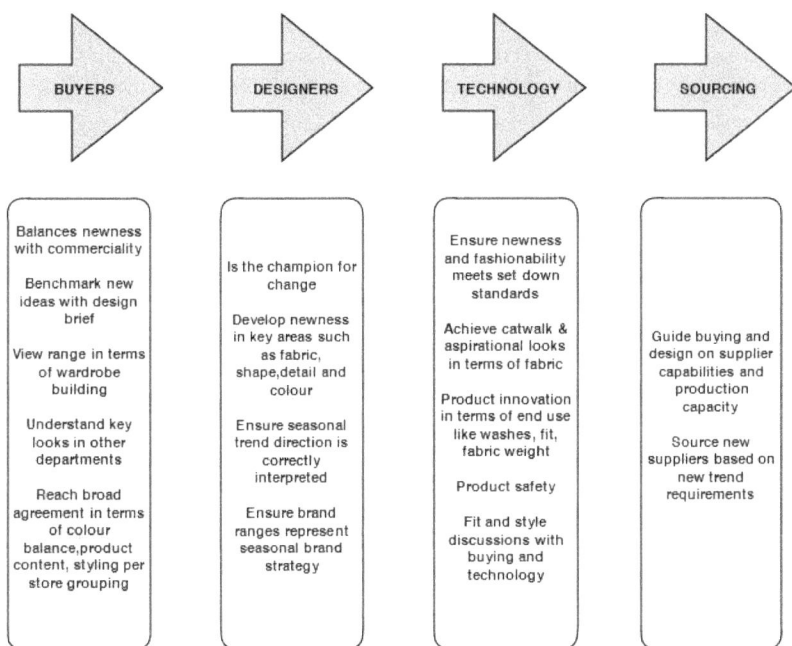

BUYERS	DESIGNERS	TECHNOLOGY	SOURCING
Balances newness with commerciality	Is the champion for change	Ensure newness and fashionability meets set down standards	Guide buying and design on supplier capabilities and production capacity
Benchmark new ideas with design brief	Develop newness in key areas such as fabric, shape,detail and colour	Achieve catwalk & aspirational looks in terms of fabric	Source new suppliers based on new trend requirements
View range in terms of wardrobe building	Ensure seasonal trend direction is correctly interpreted	Product innovation in terms of end use like washes, fit, fabric weight	
Understand key looks in other departments	Ensure brand ranges represent seasonal brand strategy	Product safety	
Reach broad agreement in terms of colour balance,product content, styling per store grouping		Fit and style discussions with buying and technology	

Suppliers are briefed and will submit appropriate samples according to the design brief pack for consideration in terms of the requirements that have emerged out of the product workshops. If the submissions are successful the samples will be finalised and accepted.

After the products are finalised, the formal contractual procurement process will commence.

VALUE ADDED PROCESSING

The need for additional work on product is frequent and the facilities to do this has to be provided for to make goods store ready. The nature of value added work can take on a variety of forms but typical examples are as follows.

Goods that are received from off shore suppliers may be bulk packed or not be received in their final form in order to achieve optimum space utilisation during transit. Prime examples of this is in the case of cushions or duvets which are space hungry but are relatively light. In order to accomplish the most efficient space usage these goods may be transported without the fibre filling or alternatively are vacuum packed. However, this operation then creates the need for additional work upon receipt to fill the cushions and unpacking of the vacuum packs as well as treating the product through pressing or steaming.

The transport of goods in cartons that eventually will be displayed on hangers, such as men's formal suits or ladies tailored garments, is done to maximise the space efficiency in containers. Upon arrival they will need to be unpacked and placed on hangers and will have to be steamed either with a hand steamer or pass through a steam tunnel. In most cases this will also require the attachment of price tickets and garment information labels.

Repackaging may be required where bulk transit quantities need to be debagged and repackaged into smaller stock room packs ready for allocation to stores.

It does happen that there may be garments received from the supplier with defects or returned from stores which are repairable in order to make them available in a saleable state which has to be done by the value-adder.

The location of the added value service provider can be either at an independent site or be incorporated in the retailer's warehouse facility. The challenge with an offsite location, particularly with the receipt of offshore product is the fact that the goods are received by another facility and reflect on a separate stock record which renders the administration of stock to be more complex.

It is preferable to have the value added processing done in the retailer's warehouse facility as there is control of the receipt of the goods and performance is more easily managed. The operation can possibly be done on a contractual basis whereby the processor rents space within the warehouse or the space is alternatively staffed with warehouse resources as a separate entity and not included in the distribution centre operational costs. It should be noted that the cost of this processing work forms part of the cost of the product and must be included in the determination of the product margin.

Building the range plan

The construction of a range plan may commence once the financial targets are available through the product and store plans together with a store catalogue matrix. The range plan enables the drafting of a so called "shopping list" for the buying team to be able to fill in the blanks as they make their selections.

The purpose of the range plan is to ensure that the offer of commercial and all-inclusive product ranges meet the needs of all customers. This is done through the combination of the elements of science which covers the planning aspect and art that represents the buying function. To expand further, the scientific practice delivers the clarity of the range offer, the quantities of style and colour levels with the correct pricing policies that support structured cataloguing which meet the varying customer profile pools. The artistic involvement delivers beautiful product and style in categories offering real choice in a way that they are easy to shop. The determination to achieve a successful balanced combination will assist in the potential maximisation of sales and profit as well as undoubtedly help to grow market share.

The philosophies of building a range is the procedure of analysing the historical sales of product categories as well as heeding the lessons learnt from previous seasons and being guided by the strategic definitions. Modifications to the current range structures could be done to compensate for missed opportunities, lost sales through uncommon adversities which should be accounted for as is the need to cater for inflated sales as a result of upcoming out of the norm special events.

Stages of building the range

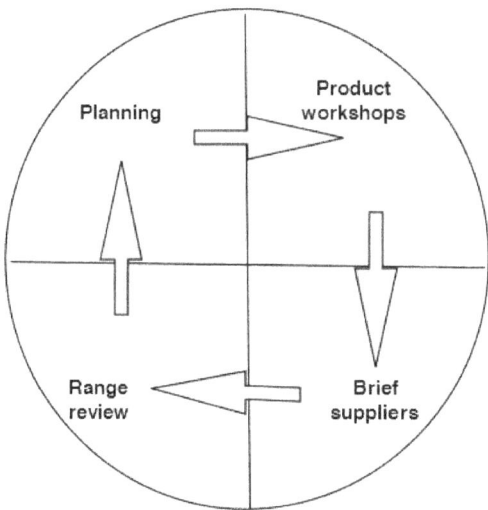

Planning begins with the range strategy document or matrix tick sheet which covers the customer choices across the period in time such as the season for six months for both the spring/summer and autumn/winter periods.

This stage is completed by the buyer and planner with reference to the group and departmental strategy.

Buyers give consideration to the historical sales, lessons learnt, customer and market shifts to determine the ideal flow of products to accommodate the continuity and input lines utilising the understanding of actual sales, customer needs and marketing plan.

Planners consider the history and lessons learnt, strategy, budgets, volumes, and the frequency of newness and catalogue shifts.

The buyers and planners then agree a final version of the range plan within the parameters of the intake budget.

Product workshops are conducted to identify the continuity items which represent the building blocks of the department, the highlighting of those products which can be seen as those that will take the department to new levels that prevent the ranges becoming stagnant, incorporating the new fashion trends which potentially could result in new shifts and ensure an appropriate level of balance between newness and traditional continuity items.

Briefing of suppliers is usually done through the compilation of a briefing pack containing quality information which enables the supplier to clearly understand the thinking of the department and get it right the first time in terms of product development. To do this effectively, the communication has to be clear and details of components, fabrics and styling features have to be simply specified. A good habit to utilise is to reference previous styles or samples.

Range reviews or final workshops are the conclusion point where the product selected is compared to the original agreed concepts and strategies to decide whether or not any changes need to be made. A cross check needs to be done to make sure that the competitive or sales environment have not altered in any significant way and plans must to be adjusted accordingly. The sequencing of the range and volumes is confirmed to ensure that all end uses are catered for, that products do not compete with each other and the categories are balanced. Lastly the range should be built from bottom up across the various groupings of stores to determine how the product will be represented across the entire chain.

The right product at the right time in the right place in the right quantities and the influences that affect these attributes is illustrated below

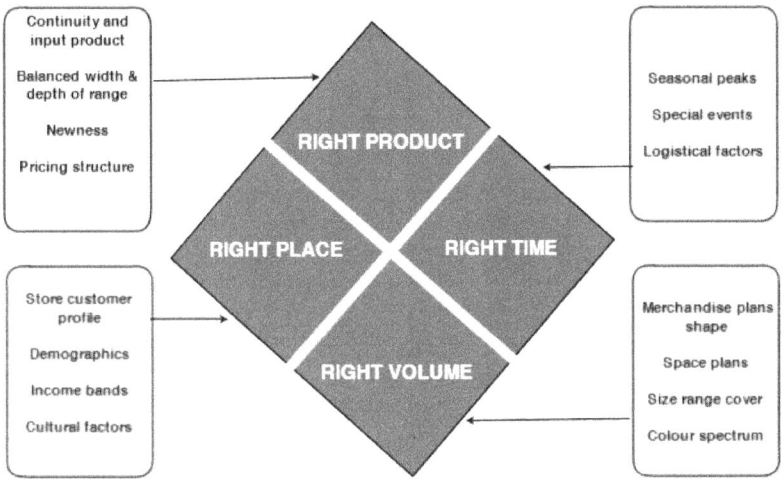

A balance of the right product mix between the basic range types and the fashion inputs has to be determined. The large volume items should be the first focus to ensure that the relevant high money takers are looked after adequately. Second is the necessity to correctly identify the characteristics of fashion forward goods for each product category in order that they best meet the respective store groupings customer profiles and reflect good relative value in comparison to other internal or external products.

The end goal is best summarised by the well-worn quote of having the right product at the right time in the right place in the right quantities.

Range presentations

It is only natural that before the final go-ahead to commit to production is given that the intended range for the forthcoming season is presented to the senior management of a retail organisation in order to get their views, buy in and sign off as a combined decision making unit.

Prior to the commencement of the season it is normal that the design team briefs management and buying groups of key looks, colour themes and other relevant trends for the forthcoming season, while the post seasonal analysis is presented by the commercial team of the buying groups to highlight some of the key lessons learnt from the previous season's trading. The commercial arm will also get approval of proposed budget levels and strategy intents from senior management to ensure that all are aligned in thinking before going ahead with the planning process and the range build.

The range presentations can take on varying formats but in the main the end objective remains the same in that all stakeholders must be comfortable with the selections and strategies to maximise the sales and profit potential.

The attendees who would participate would normally be senior management and the representatives of the relevant buying teams being the category managers, buyers, merchandisers, technologists, location planners, allocators, marketing team, store representatives, members of the design team and supply chain or logistical team members all of whom may well make contributions where appropriate.

Typical contributions are where the technologists may describe new innovations, the garment technologists or sourcing specialists could discuss supplier issues and describe new suppliers. A store representative will add comment as to possibly the practicality of styling based on what they have gleaned through their interaction with customers. Location planners will confirm that the quantities being purchased are sufficient to serve the designated catalogue or will accommodate the volumes required for planned promotions as outlined by marketing.

The agenda is usually commenced with an overall summary by the category manager of the strategy which will refer to supplier sourcing, technological developments, pricing policies, key looks and themes and lessons learnt from the previous year which have been taken on board.

The presentation of the numbers side of the department is done by the merchandiser using the line by line department summary as a point of reference. The main points that are highlighted will be the budget levels emphasising the performance in comparison to last year as well as the proportions of each product category with special attention being given to the splits between the automatic replenishment type product and the more fashionable input lines which will carry the newness and represent the more exciting part of the range.

It is usually with regard to this that some form of clarification may be required where levels tend to deviate from the norm. An example of this may well be reflected in increases that are excessive but are justified possibly by a new initiative or increase in store catalogue that is being introduced. What must be guarded against is that the level of increase of the continuity lines tends to be set more conservatively as the assumption is made that they can grow to a level which will be greater than the budget because the raw material requirement is placed ahead of time. The temptation is thereby to free up funds to enable the introduction or addition of the more fashionable product which will not be as easy to turn on. Technically if thought is applied to this practice, it is nothing else but a disguised form of over buying.

Another point needs to be made with reference to the practice of funding the input fashion lines from the surplus created by the conservative budgeting of continuity lines. If this tactic is employed it will result in the distortion of the buying margin. The reality is that the continuity lines will probably sell at higher levels than budgeted but as they carry more conservative margins the actual overall margin will be less than that which was presented.

Other aspects that will be referred to be the unit increases in relation to last year and comments will be made about the overall increase or decrease in percentage terms and differentiation will be made between the like for like product price movements which should be referenced to the current consumer price index.

The profit margins will be discussed to ensure that the profit objectives are met taking into account the levels of mark downs planned and confirming the reality of these amounts based on historical performance.

The attribute splits need to be confirmed such as short sleeves versus long sleeves, collar versus non-collar, tops compared to bottoms, colour ratios, size characteristics, woven versus knitted goods, the fabric type splits and the like.

While the number part of the meeting is often seen as the dull and boring bit with very little exciting exposure to the actual product it nevertheless remains probably the most important part of setting the business end foundation and should be given the attention to detail that is deserved.

Once the numbers have been agreed and all team members are comfortable, the buyer will proceed to present the product that is going to make up the range which is going to deliver the budgetary objectives. The most convenient way is to first display the continuity product that will flow through for the entire season and then drop in the monthly inputs which will emphasise the themes in terms of styling and colour for each relevant month. It is also important to check that the specific looks tie in with the other department's complementary product to ensure themes are aligned.

The products display the detail pertaining to the garment on an attached card such as the quantity being purchased, the catalogue of the stores that they are destined for, the selling price and margin and colours with corresponding swatches. Where possible the product should be in the actual material and make up that will be representative of what will be seen in stores. It may have to be that for product which is earmarked for a latter part of the seasons that CAD boards will have to suffice.

In the presentation of the range by month a recommended tactic would be to build the look by store catalogue where the smaller stores range will be displayed first and ticked off and then followed by what the next band of stores will receive until the full range which the flagship stores will carry is displayed. In this way the range across the full chain can be envisaged and attendees are not misled into thinking that the look of the entire range is going to all stores.

As with other meetings the conclusions should be noted, actions listed with time deadlines attached and an accountability component included. This note should be circulated to all attendees and kept on file to serve as a point of reference should there be disagreement when the actual goods reach the sales floor and they are not remembered as the same that was signed off.

Responsibilities of key presenters at a product and planning review

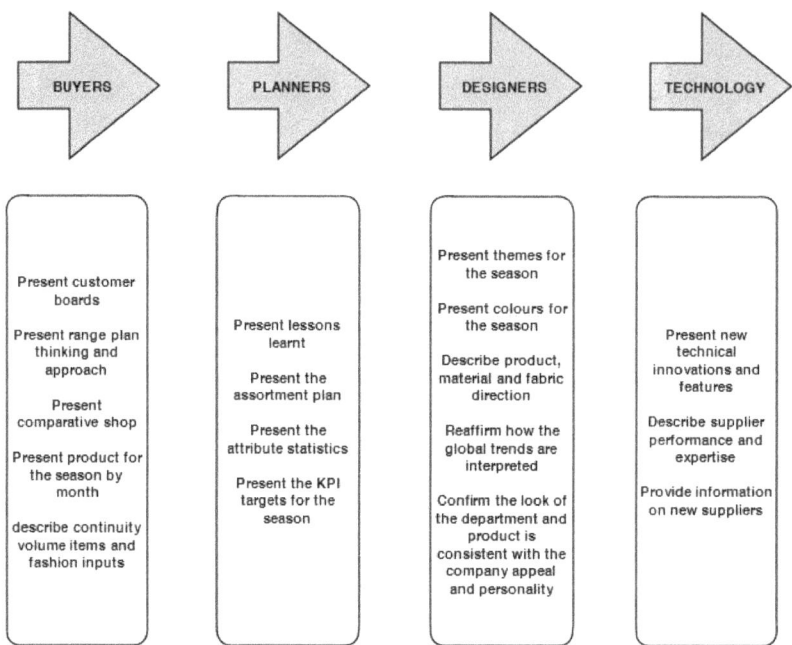

TRAINING

One of the common requirements of each role that has been outlined is that in order to achieve the highest degree of proficiency there should be a structured methodology of training which will include on the job training where the incumbent is mentored by a qualified and experienced more senior specialist who in turn has had exposure to effective training methods and performance management techniques. Ideally as the trainee progresses they will take on the responsibility for a small section of their department in order to gain the confidence and skills that will stand them in good stead going forward and also serve as a contingency in the event of the loss of senior personnel.

Coupled to on the job training is the formal classroom style lecturing as is necessary and can be performed by either internal or external tutors who will provide the theory that is matched to that which has been learnt on the job. This is of great importance as it is not uncommon that with on the job training exclusively the poor habits of the trainer are frequently transferred downwards.

Equally important is for new appointees to have an understanding and appreciation of the roles of their counterparts in other areas of the business. In order for this to be achieved they should spend adequate time attached to specialists in other fields. An example would be where a buyer in training would need to spend time in stores interacting with customers, at suppliers, with merchandisers, technologists, the marketing team and packaging specialists, in the warehouse and with the logistical experts including forwarding agents. These attachments should be well thought out with specific objectives in mind and followed up in formal reviews in front of a panel of experts from each area who test their understanding. An independent representative from human resources should also be present to ensure that the consistency of standards applied across the business is maintained and the assessment is objective without any personal bias of trainers subjectively influencing the conclusions either positively or negatively.

Overall, in order to guarantee the creation of professional teams is that the training needs to be consistent and that the outcomes deliver broadly the same standard of qualified appointees. An outstanding illustration of this is where the customer enjoys the same high level of service from sales personnel in whatever store they frequent or suppliers enjoy similar levels of proficiency across different buying teams.

Two common errors that are made which dilute the depth of knowledge is firstly, the situation where managers are appointed over areas where they have had none or very little exposure or experience. This leads to them being unable to assess the information presented with authority and makes the mentoring role required to develop juniors in some cases ineffective.

The second error that is relatively common is the assumption that because the person may be extremely proficient in performing their task it will automatically mean that they will be equally good in being the boss. The truth is that the exact reverse may well apply in that they may not have the inherent management skills and invariably will over focus on the detail and still have the desire to continue doing the work themselves.

Both such scenarios will lead to the situation where the officeholders will lose confidence in themselves and the respect of their subordinates will be weakened.

PROCESS FLOW OF KEY RETAIL ACTIVITIES

While a lot of activities are required from conceptualisation to the eventual offering of a completed product to the customer they do nevertheless follow a relative set sequence of events even though there may be at any point in time where they can possibly overlap each other.

In the sections that follow, the detail required for each key activity will be explored and their relationships and dependencies on each other will be highlighted.

The journey commences broadly with strategy formulation and the strategic planning for each stakeholder area, the creation of a merchandise plan through to the buying of the product within the budgetary parameters. The commercial team have the support of the technology teams to establish the technical requirements as well as the sourcing of appropriate suppliers in order to enable the production of the product.

The packaging is detailed to assist in the marketing of the product and protect the garments in transit and storage. Orders are initiated and the critical production milestones are managed in such a way to ensure delivery deadlines are met timeously.

During production the quality inspection and supplier performance management takes place and once the order is complete the products will be allocated and delivered either directly to stores or to a storage facility. In some instances there may be value added processes applied to the goods after which they will be transported to stores.

Once the goods are on offer to the customer the sales are analysed and reviewed in order to make adjustments where necessary. At the end of the season the lessons learnt are noted and applied to the strategy development for the new season.

The changing of the way we work

There is a well-worn saying about change and that it is certain is that there will be change. In talking about change it is unusual to understand what is unlikely to change and there are elements that will not change in the near future.

Included in these elements are items such as certainty where we know we need assurance that it is possible to avoid pain and gain pleasure. A basic need is also that we need variety to keep up the levels of stimulation through continuous change as well the desire to feel significant through recognition and develop a feeling of belonging or being loved and respected. The need to continually wishing to grow and expand our capacities and capabilities will never change and the contribution that we make will satisfy the sense of delivering to the best of our ability. Building a feeling of trust amongst all those with whom we interact is a major factor. All these elements will remain static while the environment wherein we operate will without doubt keep on changing on a continuous basis.

The way we work in the longer term is highly likely to dramatically change. There is no dispute that the manner in which tasks are completed is rapidly adapting to suit a totally new environment. The advancement of technology, connectivity and the expectations of both employers and employees are demanding that the economic activities be radically reviewed.

There is an ever increasing trend to relocate resources from the traditional high density centres such as Hong Kong, Tokyo, London, Paris and the like because of high living costs, fast increasing rentals, and salaries which are being outpaced by costs. As a result the purchasing power of residents is being severely diminished and therefore this tendency is forcing organisations to relocate to areas where it is cheaper to live and conduct business. Technology has aided this process as it is easier to operate from remoter areas and still have access through tools such as Google, Dropbox, Skype and the like which makes it just as easy to service customers as effectively no matter where the base location is. The base link ups could also be temporary in that desks could be rented with all the required technological facilities, boardroom or conference facilities supported by the appropriate equipment and catering requirements thus saving investment in permanent structures.

During some of my research, I came across an article written by Robert M. Goldman MD, PhD, DO, FAASP that had such an impact on me in terms of the illustration as to what has happened and what potentially can happen in our world, I felt it best be presented verbatim to maximise the message.

FUTURE PREDICTIONS

In 1998, Kodak had 170,000 employees and sold 85% of all photo paper worldwide. Within just a few years, their business model disappeared and they went bankrupt. What happened to Kodak will happen in a lot of industries in the next 10 years - and most people don't see it coming. Did you think in 1998 that 3 years later you would never take pictures on paper film again? Yet digital cameras were invented in 1975. The first ones only had 10,000 pixels, but followed Moore's law. So as with all exponential technologies, it was a disappointment for a long time, before it became way superior and got mainstream in only a few short years. It will now happen with Artificial Intelligence, health, autonomous and electric cars, education, 3D printing, agriculture and jobs. Welcome to the 4th Industrial Revolution. Welcome to the Exponential Age.

Software will disrupt most traditional industries in the next 5-10 years.
Uber is just a software tool, they don't own any cars, and are now the biggest taxi company in the world. Airbnb is now the biggest hotel company in the world, although they don't own any properties.

Artificial Intelligence: Computers become exponentially better in understanding the world. This year, a computer beat the best Go player in the world, 10 years earlier than expected. In the US, young lawyers already don't get jobs. Because of IBM Watson, you can get legal advice (so far for more or less basic stuff) within seconds, with 90% accuracy compared with 70% accuracy when done by humans. So if you study law, stop immediately. There will be 90% fewer lawyers in the future, only specialists will remain. Watson already helps nurses diagnosing cancer, 4 time more accurate than human nurses. Facebook now has a pattern recognition software that can recognize faces better than humans. By 2030, computers will become more intelligent than humans.

Autonomous Cars: In 2018 the first self-driving cars will appear for the public. Around 2020, the complete industry will start to be disrupted. You don't want to own a car anymore. You will call a car with your phone, it will show up at your location and drive you to your destination. You will not need to park it, you only pay for the driven distance and can be productive while driving. Our kids will never get a driver's license and will never own a car. It will change the cities, because we will need 90-95% fewer cars for that. We can transform former parking space into parks. 1.2 million people die each year in car accidents worldwide. We now have one accident every 100,000 km, with autonomous driving that will drop to one accident in 10 million km. That will save a million lives each year.

Most car companies may become bankrupt. Traditional car companies try the evolutionary approach and just build a better car, while tech companies (Tesla, Apple, Google) will do the revolutionary approach and build a computer on wheels. I spoke to a lot of engineers from Volkswagen and Audi; they are completely terrified of Tesla.

Insurance Companies will have massive trouble because without accidents, the insurance will become 100x cheaper. Their car insurance business model will disappear.

Real estate will change. Because if you can work while you commute, people will move further away to live in a more beautiful neighbourhood.

Electric cars won't become mainstream until 2020. Cities will be less noisy because all cars will run on electric. Electricity will become incredibly cheap and clean: Solar production has been on an exponential curve for 30 years, but you can only now see the impact. Last year, more solar energy was installed worldwide than fossil. The price for solar will drop so much that all coal companies will be out of business by 2025.

With cheap electricity comes cheap and abundant water. Desalination now only needs 2kWh per cubic meter. We don't have scarce water in most places, we only have scarce drinking water. Imagine what will be possible if anyone can have as much clean water as he wants, for nearly no cost.

Health: There will be companies that will build a medical device (called the "Tricorder" from Star Trek) that works with your phone, which takes your retina scan, your blood sample and you breathe into it. It then analyses 54 biomarkers that will identify nearly any disease. It will be cheap, so in a few years everyone on this planet will have access to world class medicine, nearly for free.

3D printing: The price of the cheapest 3D printer came down from $18,000 to $400 within 10 years. In the same time, it became 100 times faster. All major shoe companies started 3D printing shoes. Spare airplane parts are already 3D printed in remote airports. The space station now has a printer that eliminates the need for the large number of spare parts they used to have in the past.

At the end of this year, new smart phones will have 3D scanning possibilities. You can then 3D scan your feet and print your perfect shoe at home. In China, they already 3D printed a complete 6-storey office building. By 2027, 10% of everything that's being produced will be 3D printed.

Business Opportunities: If you think of a niche you want to go in, ask yourself: "in the future, do you think we will have that?" and if the answer is yes, how can you make that happen sooner? If it doesn't work with your phone, forget the idea. And any idea designed for success in the 20th century is doomed in to failure in the 21st century.

Work: 70-80% of jobs will disappear in the next 20 years. There will be a lot of new jobs, but it is not clear if there will be enough new jobs in such a small time.

Agriculture: There will be a $100 agricultural robot in the future. Farmers in 3rd world countries can then become managers of their field instead of working all days on their fields. Agroponics will need much less water. The first Petri dish produced veal is now available and will be cheaper than cow-produced veal in 2018. Right now, 30% of all agricultural surfaces is used for cows. Imagine if we don't need that space anymore. There are several startups that will bring insect protein to the market shortly. It contains more protein than meat. It will be labelled as "alternative protein source" (because most people still reject the idea of eating insects).

There is an app called "moodies" which can already tell in which mood you are. Until 2020 there will be apps that can tell by your facial expressions if you are lying. Imagine a political debate where it's being displayed when they are telling the truth and when not.

Bitcoin will become mainstream this year and might even become the default reserve currency.

Longevity: Right now, the average life span increases by 3 months per year. Four years ago, the life span used to be 79 years, now it's 80 years. The increase itself is increasing and by 2036, there will be more than one year increase per year. So we all might live for a long long time, probably way more than 100.

Education: The cheapest smart phones are already at $10 in Africa and Asia. Until 2020, 70% of all humans will own a smart phone. That means, everyone has the same access to world class education.

Robert M. Goldman MD, PhD, DO, FAASP
www.DrBobGoldman.com
World Chairman-International Medical Commission
Co-Founder & Chairman of the Board-A4M
Founder & Chairman-International Sports Hall of Fame
Co-Founder & Chairman-World Academy of Anti-Aging Medicine
President Emeritus-National Academy of Sports Medicine (NASM)
Chairman-U.S. Sports Academy's Board of Visitors

Apart from being able to conveniently work from different sites the necessity for a substantial portion of the workforce no longer have to negotiate the traffic or use public transport daily and therefore the surplus time saving can be productively utilised. There are instances that those firms who find it difficult to adapt to this newer culture and stubbornly maintain a level of mistrust have experienced a depletion of suitable staff and productivity as the workforce prefer to pursue a flexible option. It is important that the mind shift of acknowledging that the quality delivery of tasks should be the measure of productivity and not the actual time spent in the office.

The trend has evolved that an incumbent is no longer a specialist in one field all their life. With the ongoing development of new processes, technologies and systems in order to be successful there is a continual need for education and re-education. One big degree for a lifelong job at one corporation is being replaced by a culture of a repeatable cycle of learning then work, then learn again and work to sustain competitiveness in the labour market. It is fact that where in the past job hopping carried a considerable stigma, this is now more than ever becoming the norm.

In days gone by, the evidence of consistent job hopping on an applicant's resume hinted that in all likelihood presented a negative perception that the candidate probably had a people issue and did not get on with others, could not hold down a job, was disloyal and could not commit to a long term relationship.

The reality is that the opposite is becoming the actuality especially with regard to advancing through a continual learning and relearning process and the new job hopping millennia's are now perceived to possess a higher learning curve, perform better and deliver above expectations as they pursue the drive to make a favourable impression and assert themselves in a shorter time period with each employer.

Because such employees are continually challenging themselves outside their comfort zones they are typically over achievers who deliver a significant contribution to the bottom line which stands them in good stead before they move on to new opportunities every two to four years. It is believed that the learning curve tends to flatten after three years so in fact regular job hopping has become crucial to ensure a stable career growth.

It nevertheless can remain a concern for companies as there is a continual requirement to invest in new staff but the upside is that the rapid growth of the organisation and the worry of the loss of intellectual property to competitors is less threatening because the swift change makes the impact of the loss of such intellectual assets soon to be outdated.

The world is also seeing an exponential growth of entrepreneurs who with their specialised knowledge, offer their services on a short term basis simply by working as freelancers or contractors. With a wide-ranging exposure they enhance their skills and are thereby able to raise their rates or acquire additional freelancers to assist them and consequently grow their personal wealth.

The organisational structure
The basic hierarchical staffing roles of all the key players in a mainstream buying structure is outlined as follows.

The chief executive officer is clearly the leader together with the board of directors who ensure that the overall company strategic intent is delivered and the profits are achieved as reward to the shareholders to whom they are accountable.

Group executives look after the broad category types such as menswear, ladieswear and childrenswear. The responsibility is to ensure that the group delivers to the set strategy and is reacting properly to changing trading conditions while still meeting the profit objective.

Within the mainstream groups such as menswear a sub division into sub groups may well take place probably by lifestyle like formal wear and casual wear. The category manager is responsible for the mini business or sub group with set turnover targets, profit objectives and strategies.

Buyers, merchandisers and location planners operate at the departmental level down to the lowest degree of product being colour and size and are responsible that the management of the detail delivers the eventual goals at all the higher levels.

It must be emphasised that there is a very definitive collaborative process between the buying and merchandising team where an appropriate measure of tension may exist. The same environment may apply between the finance departments and the buying team in terms of the financial budget.

Key staffing hierarchy posts of the buying organisation are illustrated below

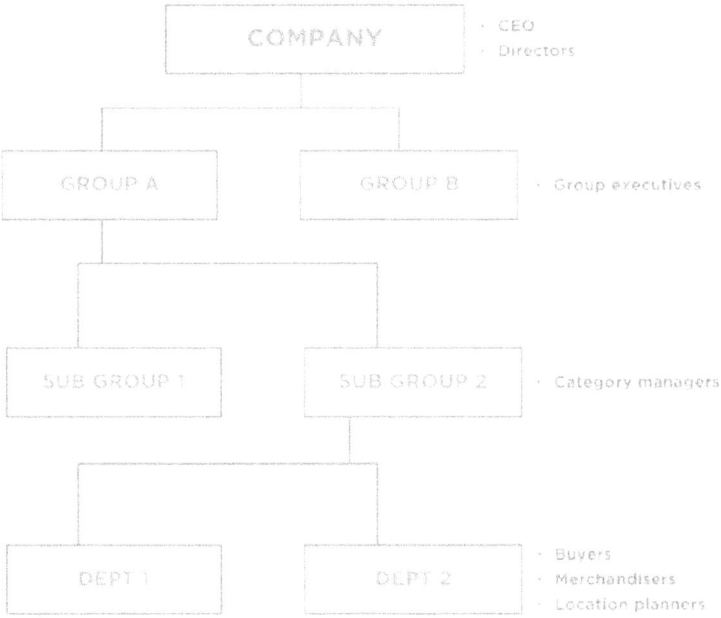

Product planning

Once there is a clear understanding of what operational activities are required, the plan of action can be outlined to deliver the strategic objectives and thereby satisfy the goals of the strategy in the most effective way.

What is key in formulating the planning strategy is to set down the clear guidelines in the development of the product mix which will be carefully tailored in the right proportions in order to best serve the customer at the various locations and in terms of styling, colour quantities across the sizes at the most acceptable prices.

For this to be done successfully the overall process of planning follows a set of prescribed activities that make up the mechanics of running the business as well as accommodating the other stakeholder strategies. The steps are a flow of taking in the lessons learnt during the previous season and utilising the learnings as input in the formulation of the strategic goals for the future season.

The goals will give guidance in the preparation of the level of budgets determining the product mix and setting up the range plan from which the orders will be placed. Once production has taken place according to the plan the goods will be allocated to the stores taking into account their specific customer characteristics. Sales will be analysed as they occur and as the performance dictates the forward plans will be reviewed and adjusted appropriately.

Diagrammatically the high level key planning steps can be outlined as follows

No matter how much time and thought is spent in drafting the strategy and planning forecast it is inevitable that the reality will deviate from what is expected as a result of the volatile internal and external factors that exist at the time. Therefore it is critical to continually review actual performance, analyse the trends and take appropriate action to minimise the risks. Where adjustments are not able to be made to remedy a situation the lessons learnt must be taken on board and banked to be avoided in future trading seasons.

The path to follow in the process of comparing the actual performance in relation to the plan can be outlined as follows

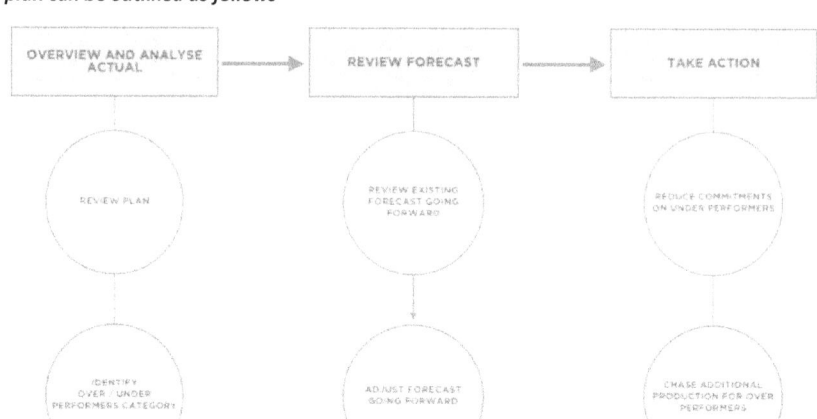

The start point of analysing and comparing the actual performance to the intended plan at a point in time, is to firstly to compare actual sales to date at total departmental level and drill down to product level and based on the result, review the planned sales for the balance of the season.

The potential new sales forecast is then compared to the actual commitment of product in the form of stock on hand at stores, product in transit and that at the supplier as well as the orders in the pipeline to determine the resultant shortage or surplus of stock.

The procedure which needs to be followed can be broken down into three distinct activities.

The recording of the total plan for the season in terms of sales and the planned breaking stocks at the end of the season as well as the current week's performance which has just been completed.

Based on the comparison of the actual sales to date in relation to that which was budgeted for may require a review of the balance of sales to be achieved and thereby create a revised forecast for the total season. The change in the sales forecast may also then require an adaptation of the planned breaking stocks to reflect the reality of the sales plan.

Once the realistic revised sales performance has been established, the result then needs to be compared to the total stock commitment and assessed whether there is sufficient stock in the pipeline to achieve the revised targets. If this is not the case, a plan has to be devised in order to determine what action is required to achieve this or conversely there may be a consequent surplus of stock which will have to be reduced.

Believe it or not the start of planning for a forthcoming season begins with what has happened in the past.

A strategic focus in the assessment of the past performance for the season is to compare the actual vital numbers to that what was expected and understand the deviations whether they were positive or negative. The learnings are imperative in the compilation of a new season's strategy and the setting of targets.

Once there is a clear understanding of what operational activities are required, the plan of action can be outlined to deliver the strategic objectives and thereby satisfy the goals of the strategy in the most effective way.

What is key in formulating the planning strategy is to set down the clear guidelines in the development of the product mix which will be carefully tailored in the right proportions in order to best serve the customer at the various locations and in terms of styling, colour quantities across the sizes at the most acceptable prices.

For this to be done successfully the overall process of planning follows a set of prescribed activities that make up the mechanics of running the business as well as accommodating the other stakeholder strategies. The steps are a flow of taking in the lessons learnt during the previous season and utilising the learnings as input in the formulation of the strategic goals for the future season.

The goals will give guidance in the preparation of the level of budgets determining the product mix and setting up the range plan from which the orders will be placed. Once production has taken place according to the plan the goods will be allocated to the stores taking into account their specific customer characteristics.

CONCLUSION

In the evaluation of the varying roles and the integration of the individual activities the deduction is clearly evident that in order to ensure that there is a successfull aligned team exertion requires complete understanding and respect for each others chunks with all interaction being done maturely and sensibly in order that the achievement of the overall common strategic goals are maximised.

www.ingramcontent.com/pod-product-compliance
Lightning Source LLC
Chambersburg PA
CBHW070727180526
45167CB00004B/1646